A HARD SUMMATION

Also by Afaa Michael Weaver

Water Song
Some Days It's A Slow Walk to Evening
My Father's Geography
Stations in a Dream
Timber and Prayer
Talisman
The Ten Lights of God
Sandy Point
Multitudes
The Plum Flower Dance
The Government of Nature
City of Eternal Spring

A HARD SUMMATION

poems

Afaa Michael Weaver

CENTRAL SQUARE PRESS

Copyright © 2014 by Afaa Michael Weaver.

All rights reserved. No part of this book may be used or reproduced in any manner whatsoever without written permission from the publisher, except in the case of brief quotations embodied in critical articles or reviews.

All inquiries and permissions requests should be addressed to the Publisher:
Central Square Press
P.O. Box 2621
Lynn, MA 01903

publisher@centralsquarepress.com
www.centralsquarepress.com

Published in the United States of America
First Edition

ISBN-13: 978-1-941604-00-7

ISBN-10: 1941604005

Thank you to the editors of the following print and online publications in which these poems first appeared:

The Writer's Chronicle: "In Charleston, the Slave Market," "The Kidnappers," "Night Song for Missy," "The Pearl and Uncle Tom's Cabin"; Barrow Street: "Moms Mabley Runs a Boston at the Nid Whist Table in North Philly, 1945," "The Little Rock Nine," "On the Passing of Heaven Sutton."

Cover art: "When the family moved to new orleans" © Najee Dorsey.

Cover design: Lila Khan

to The Kenosha Congress of Poets for Peace
and The City of Kenosha, Wisconsin

CONTENTS

Introduction by Enzo Silon Surin   IX

The Kidnappers   3
A Ship's Log   4
In Charleston, the Slave Market   6
Night Song for Missy   8
The Pearl and Uncle Tom's Cabin   10
Harvesting the Saints   11
Migration, the Big Cities   13
Black Star Line, 1925   15
Butterbeans and Susie, a Depression Duet   17
Moms Mabley Runs a Boston at the Bid Whist Table in North Philly, 1945   19
The Little Rock 9   21
After Civil Rights, Disaster Came   26
On the Passing of Heaven Sutton   27

Notes   29
About the Author   32

INTRODUCTION

It is not by accident that the poems in this chapbook are numbered in thirteen. Thirteen. A prime number, only divisible by one and itself. Prime also because it represents the first year a child enters into the middle passage of its teen years. Thirteen. As in the thirteen original colonies, symbolizing rebirth and independence. Thirteen. As in the thirteenth amendment, abolishing slavery and involuntary servitude...except as punishment for a crime—historically, *being black*. Thirteen. As in the thirteenth section of Thirteen Ways at Looking at a Blackbird (Wallace Stevens). Thirteen. As in t'hurt-teen. Thirteen. A sign of misfortune, of horror, the sum of nightmares, a bad omen's bad omen.

A HARD SUMMATION is a suite of 13 new poems by Afaa Michael Weaver, covering the history of African Americans from the Middle Passage to Now. Like a rite of passage, struggle has been unyielding and synonymous with the black experience in America. In this rich compilation, Weaver unearths a genealogical deficit that permeates through generations.

But in this collection, you won't hear the poems cry foul or attempt to appease friend or offend foe. Its intention is hardly to be conclusive. When you add it all up, A HARD SUMMATION offers us an opportunity to listen, celebrate, commemorate, and appreciate the successes and failures of the past in order to develop a current and contextual understanding of what it means to be Black and American.

—*Enzo Silon Surin*, Publisher

A HARD SUMMATION

The Kidnappers

A cruel silence in the night, the children's songs
pulled under a rustle of leaves, mothers turning away
for a second to pick up toys dropped in shadows,
as hands cover children's mouths, their heels
struggling in soft dirt, swallowed by forests,
birth turned to death, the yard empty, neighbors
hushed by wailing from houses where ache lives,
a cruel silence in the night, the children's songs
gone, mama pulled into the broad arms of papa,
dry womb of old sinew and bone, eyes glazed,
sons and daughters, hope against old age, swept up
by strangers to lie down in the music of deep water.

A Ship's Log

Children who gave us life...
a family's seed on board the Jesus Maria
Who took you? Sherbro Mende Portuguese?
Who took your name to your mother's ears
to whisper, child gone, womb of your grandchildren
gone? Who set you free in Havana? What filled you
in the ship of two hundred thirty-four mostly children,
half of them boys, half of them girls, eight, nine, ten
years into a language they will forget, what happened
to the crew listening to children cry for weeks
from Freetown to Havana, Freetown where slaves
begin...and did the crisp light of the moon curse sailors
who waited to ease below to prowl and touch at night?
Children...a ship full of mothers screaming where
these could not hear their names being cried out,
girls and boys shivering in the creak of wood
in the water, the forward dip and lean of sail to wind,
their names being cried out in languages they will barely
know if they live to think of what they know...ribbed
womb of ship belly, plank to plank, cog and nail, cupped
hands of demons moving in the Atlantic to progress
with children whose names have kept their power—

Mamboa Bunde Sulu Guebo Mafoma Janu
Boya   Daru   Maju Cobre Mafe   Ita
Dora   Duevo Maqueni Momo Manene Canundi
Cumba Guenda Iacaye Sese Beilu Colloma

sons and daughters, hope against old age, swept up
by strangers to lie down in the music of deep water,
a baptism in a melody of grief, the children praying
to be loved in a world their mothers do not know
in Africa where stars try to make peace with death

In Charleston, the Slave Market

A mother speaks to a dream that speaks to her
on an Igbo bed, tell me where my children are,
she asks of the air that makes itself a door
beyond the door over the last touch, the last
smell of her children's hair full of sun, speckled
with dirt from playing, how do they eat now?
she asks of the dream, but the dream is too kind
to tell the truth, the markets where they stand naked,
white women poking at them, looking over places
only mothers should touch, shopping for black pets
for white children, for girls who can grow and make
more black children, as if they are gardens, and what
gardens they are to a mother on her Igbo bed who asks
her husband, old man who cannot make children,
what do we do? shall we stop speaking? The dream
dries itself up, pulls away so grief can become death
and kindness to hearts too full to sleep, and they
sleep the sleep of wind over wild grass, the moon
over impotent prayers, the wild sounds of angels and
hyenas, they sleep until sleep is all there is, the grace
of the end of wondering, while in Charleston one child
is sold here, one child there, one swimming leagues

down under in the dark tongue of the ocean where
thunderheads in Charleston harbor cannot send the rain.

mama's little baby got some something
mama's little baby got a sweet potato pie
mama's little baby got some something
mama's little baby got a hot butter biscuit
gonna bring it to you mama, right now

Night Song for Missy

My bones tied up with his bones at night,
him falling asleep in my arm after wrasslin me,
calling it love in some kind of low whisper
no dog would believe. I know his every smell,
every way the littlest corner of him be stinkin
underneath me, on top of me, while our children
snore in the corner, then he creep out the way
he creep in, before the cock crow at the sun.

In daylight he act like we strangers, on the edge
of the field, his little tan children of mine turning
brown, playing more than working cause they his
children, Missy look over at me while I look
over at her, both of us got some kind of papers
on this same man that say he own both of us,
the man who owes us even when he die cause
the Bible say you gotta look after the widow.

But when he die it will be cause Missy and me
locked eyes many days and hated him like one
wronged woman made out of two, him standing
up there on the porch studyin everything--
his eyes lit up like he the Lord of all creation.

hush now, night wind on my skin, hush now
bird lost in trees, hush now, hungry moon

The Pearl and Uncle Tom's Cabin

In the drop of the anchor into the bay, the ripplng waves,
a hundred flowers blooming fell, canaries choked in caves.

Mothers lost their children's crosses, Jesus found a grave,
a place where preacher songs and prayers made us slaves.

They brought us back to Washington, captain, crew, and guests,
to wait in jails for auctioneers to see which punishment was best.

In a single day we failed, the ship sailed no farther away
than lines the sea makes under the sun on Chesapeake Bay.

Had the word been kept more silent and lips tightly bound,
night could have been longer and landed us on freer ground.

If the wind had been stronger, if the ship had sailed,
we would have been slave no longer and freedom prevailed.

Harvesting the Saints

When winter come early, the tree limbs
                              bout frozen
they hang stiff like the limbs, creakin sometimes
the way trees do
         and they feel like wood when they been hangin
for a little while,
              but the smell bring you back to truth.

        We brought ole James home to his wife
                      she sittin up
in her chair as quiet as the way night settle sometime,
knowing full well her husband gone, hanged
              for messin with a white woman
he never even seen,
     the devil workin that way, in the unseen world,
invisible the way Rev. Tillman always used to say
before we had to let him down from the trees
                                   one night.

I come home and count the children
         the way
I would if there was twenty of them

       instead of two,
               I count their toes and their fingers,
I count their eyes
    and they laugh at me,
                   Mama you know we got two eyes
I tell em I know they do but I need to see them eyes
all the time, and when my husband a little late
                 at night
I count the whispers the wind make
    in the window
I pretend I ain't scared and play games with the children
    until I see his eyes ease around the edge of the door.

Some of the white folk smile when the lynchin comes,
as if it's time to weigh in and see what we owe them.
Other white folk be shiverin and shakin, wipin tears
cause they know Satan's kingdom gonna fall one day.

Migration, the Big Cities

I
> –wife to husband

In the steam from the pots and the dusty air
I saw his face for the first time away from home,
away from the old country place where a pair
of old shoes and worn out hems and sweaty foam

of mules plopping around in the tobacco fields,
chickens pecking at old hardened corn on grounds
made up of "I'm alright right now" all had to yield
to "come see about me" when the little mounds

of sorrow came from having a whole lot of nothin
came to be not enough for us, the young ones
who got news of electric fans, and even somethin
we could call a living wage for daughters and sons

what grew up swallowing hope with the taste
of worrying bout honey brown gone to waste.

II
>   –husband to wife

Steelworker now, ain't no farmer no more,
met my wife in the mills, not a juke joint floor,
I got a time clock to punch and work shoes, too,
no mule to prance behind and feed hay to chew.

My dreams touch the sky and tickle heaven
as we forget night riders and the evils of men,
while we save money for our own little house
where we can feed our children a plate of souse.

I don't miss the farm and the sheriff's fine
my mama and daddy thought would be mine,
cause the A.M.E. church gave us a front pew
reserved for colored folk citified and new.

When love let loose and the children came,
we made them a space all cleared of shame
so they could know how the soul should feel
without the weight of the white man's heel.

Black Star Line, 1925
> "I was not made to be whipped…"
> –Marcus Garvey

I keep telling these children to pick up behind themselves,
to rise and give the glory to He that made the world and us,
and here I am cleaning up behind them again, we gotta get
to the UNIA meeting today, gotta get all this mess together,
Lord, a woman's work is always forever and everywhere—

>   rise up, you lowly people, rise up

Made three custard pies last night for church, got two shirts
to sew up, husband done busted them loose again, more man
than shirt, I tell him, and he just smile cause he knows he
more man than a lot of things, even when he have to bow
his head—

>   rise up, you lowly people, rise up

When it come time to rest, I just sit in the middle
of all this mess, clothes I told them to pick up, a shoe
over here that belong with a shoe over there, a glass
of precious ice water to drink after we cleaned

the plates so clean we just sat there and laughed
together, looking at the table we bought on time—

        rise up, you lowly people, rise up

Gloria came by here the other night with Peace Mission
news, Father Divine this, and Father Divine that, hosanna,
but in this house we see the whole black world rising up,
all of us like a late crop what done come to the sunlight
to be born with businesses and ocean liners of our own,
to go back to where the old folks was born and kidnapped,
cause Africa ain't no dream no more, we are goin home—

        rise up, you lowly people, rise up

Butterbeans and Susie, a Depression Duet

Papa Ain't No Santa Claus

Hard as I work, draggin myself up and down the stairs
to the subway, stairs to the bus, stairs to the job and back,
pennies for a thousand drops of sweat, and smiles
to give back to frowns, hard as I work you spend it.

Where would it all go, I wonder, if I didn't have you,
with all these little mouths like birds in a nest while
I struggle through the air, but if I could really fly,
I'd do a whole set of circle turns toward another sky.

Somewhere there must be a place without race,
where I can get up and get our necessaries and not
have to face a hammer made out of nastiness just
for me, just to weigh me down when I want to sing.

Hard as I work, draggin myself up and down the stairs,
pennies for a thousand drops of sweat, and smiles
to give back to frowns, hard as I work you spend it,
on the subway and the bus just to buy somethin new.

Mama Ain't No Christmas Tree

It takes more than a notion and some lotion to soothe
two tired feet, two feet that cook and stand all day,
hover over by the window watching the children play,
one hand on a soup spoon the other held up to pray.

I got three thousand plans for fixing up this place,
new dishes and silverware, but in the store all I see
is what the children need, what other little miracle
will make them forget the smile missin from my face.

It ain't a day goes by standin in white folks' stores
when I don't wish for that dress or patent leather gloves,
a bottle of Rigaud perfume to surprise my sweet man
at night, and you the only man I know, tight as you be.

It takes more than a notion and some lotion to soothe
me hoverin by the window, watchin the children play,
one hand on a soup spoon, the other held up to pray,
two tired feet, two feet that that cook and stand all day.

Moms Mabley Runs a Boston at the Bid Whist Table in North Philly, 1945

Bring it all to Moms, every book is mine,
just the way we took down discrimination
in the army of the USA, bring it all to me.

I know every suit in every hand, every trick
you want to play on me, bring what Moms
already see, the hearts or whatever it be.

Every train comin to my station,
every passenger, all the ticket money
comes to my Bid Whist Jubilee.

We took down the Jim Crow army
so the pullman porters can run the trains
and we be the big shots on aeroplanes.

This card table is mine all night long
cause ain't nary one of y'all got a chance.
Ole Moms gonna strut and do her dance.

You got a low, but I got the high,
while my Jokers keep your trumps in line
and give the Klu Klux Klan some jail time.

I come up from Brevard, North Carolina,
where the bedbugs have college degrees
to Philly to lift all y'all up off your knees.

First you gots to give Moms what's hers,
this hand and all the rest, matter of fact--
I'll take you and your bank book, too.

The Little Rock 9

It is Monday, I am twelve years old,
summer still feel like summer to me...

                    Ernest Green

My elementary school principal was white
I only had one white teacher, she was named
after the juice the astronauts took into space,
Tang, I got some Tang at home...did you hear
about the little girls who got killed while we was
in Sunday School yesterday?

                    Elizabeth Eckford

I live in Baltimore and so do you,
your people the raw and stinky crew,
my daddy a big shot on the Avenue
your daddy can't buy a pair of shoes...

                    Jefferson Thomas

One little girl was named Addie Mae,
just like my aunt from South Carolina,
and when I come home from church
everybody was cryin about the news
from Alabama...I know Alabama
Alabama was on the math test today—

>If you going 65 miles an hour leaving
>Richmond near where my cousins live
>and you drive for twelve hours straight
>will get you to Alabama? hell no, cause
>Alabama in hell ...

Terrence Roberts

The bus is hot, the white neighborhood
full of angry faces just two miles from where
we live, angry faces I see at night when I look
out the window and wonder why I have to sit
next to white children to be smart...I was smart
all the time, my mama told me so when I did
things the right way, extra things, good things,
smart is knowin when somethin's missing...

Carlotta Walls LaNier

I like Malcolm X because he looks like me
when I am so mad I can't stand myself, when
my cousins take my model car shelf down,
break up my cars and then dare me to fight,
when I have to walk from the white school
home through the white neighborhood when
I miss the bus or when I get a beatin for what
my friend did and he get a beatin, too, but
mine hurt more because he did it, not me, so
I like Malcolm X. He so mean, Mr. Green,
he so mean...you got to be mean in Chicago...

                        Minnijean Brown

When I was fourteen a boy kissed me
when we were walking to the movies,
he sneaked me, and I tried not to smile
because kissing is a sin and all the while
I was so full of hallelujah on the inside,
on the way to the movies we go to now
because somebody made a way somehow,
standing in lines with protest signs, dogs
barking all around, so I make sure I sound
educated when Henry sneaks to kiss me

on the way to the movies...we have
all kinds of movies in Philadelphia...

>Gloria Ray Karlmark

New York is faster than yesterday,
been here and gone before you remember
it ain't here no more, we go downtown
in the middle of tomorrow when it still be
today, New York is faster than yesterday,
I got a quarter for your ten dollar bill,
give it to me I'll pay your cleaners bill
because New York is faster than yesterday,
and a high school diploma is all a genius
like me will ever need in a city where
a thrill is more to me if you will believe
me...and believe me you will...

>Thelma Mothershed

What a word will do, my mama used to say
at night when her work was done, rearing back
in that chair of hers with the stuffin fallin out
of the arms, what a word will do when you know

what words are for, she would say, layin her head
back, closing her eyes and settling down
inside some dream. She never told us her dreams
when we asked her, she just said we would know
when the moon turned over three times and ghosts
rose up out of the sea. Mama was half out
of this world, in California we all the way in it...

                        Melba Patillo Beals

> Little Rock Nine,
> Shaking the line
> Between white no
> And black oh yes,
> I'll walk all over
> What is mine, thanks
> To Little Rock Nine.

After Civil Rights, Disaster Came

in the clang of metal doors to factories being locked in Detroit
and Baltimore, the small rings of rust growing on the tools
a capella gospel getting to be old fashioned, grandmamas
making quilts for Dr. King, grandchildren forgetting his name
in the last move up north to cities where the jobs were slow ones
in fast food places, fried chicken clogging up folks' arteries,
preachers building churches bigger than what heaven s'posed to be
young men selling drugs to each other, gunfire a wild jazz at night
America's classic music overshadowed by hiphop, rap—
uneducated anger everywhere while a false kindness
shrank the future in a concentrated hushing done in clinics
that planned our families, we the survivors of children
stolen over the Atlantic, brought to the Americas as slaves—

Mamboa   Bunde   Sulu   Guebo   Mafoma   Janu
Boya   Daru   Maju   Cobre   Mafe   Ita
Dora   Duevo   Maqueni Momo   Manene   Canundi
Cumba   Guenda Iacaye   Sese   Beilu   Colloma

On the Passing of Heaven Sutton

In the year the Mayans said our world ends,
I sit in my basement apartment, The Cave,
my neighbors from lives different from mine.

It is a most peculiar way to be sixty, up here
from down south, no way to know where up is,
what up is or should be, only what it used to be.

Winters in Boston go inside my bones until
I feel the center of nothing, where people
grow old singing Shine on Me in a capella.

It is the center of alien coldness, hearts naked
to ice, to a blank sun, a nakedness that says it is
the only choice, one that owns love's essence.

I am black because I enter that space, people
see I am the door to what they ache to know,
the long corridors and rooms of our freedom,

a place where I refuse to be told I cannot dream
my own dreams, a place where people like me
agree to offer love from an uneasy forgiveness.

Nights become deep stillness, I do a soul dance
with ancestors building a respite from history,
arguing against the hard summation of slavery,

the truth of our black wish for humanity, a seed
made from resistance, bright moments where
we teach America the song of our right to live.

Notes

1. The names in "A Ship's Log" were taken from the logs of the ship Jesus Maria, which set sail from Freetown in 1840 and landed in Havana on December 29th of that year. On the Trans-Atlantic Slave Trade Database it is voyage # 2071. Children were 98.3% of the human cargo. The ship was freed in Havana. The captain was Lorenzo Ruiz. www.slavevoyages.org

2. The Pearl Incident involved an aborted atempt by 77 slaves in 1848 to escape from Washington, D.C. Paul Jennings, a former slave who had served President James Madison, helped plan the escape. The Pearl Incident inspired Harriet Breecher Stowe, author of Uncle Tom's Cabin.

3. "Harvesting the Saints" refers to black victims of lynching in the United States. Estimates of the number of victims varies.

4. "Migration, the Big Cities," refers to the Great Migration of the twentieh century where blacks left the south in large numbers.

5. Of all the black leaders in the twentieth century, Marcus Garvey of Jamaica (1887-1940) had the most followers. His plans included establishing global businesses for blacks. His

Black Star Line was to be his shipping business, and he supported a "Back to Africa" program for resettling black people in the Motherland.

6. Butterbeans and Susie (Jodie Edwards 1895-1967 and Sue Hawthorne Edwards 1896-1963) were performers who worked as a couple in the first half of the twentieth century. They mentored younger performers such as Jackie "Moms" Mabley.

7. "Papa Ain't No Santa Claus, and Mama Ain't No Christmas Tree" is the title of a performance routine by Butterbeans and Susie.

8. Jackie "Moms" Mabley (Loretta Mary Aiken 1894-1975) was a comedian and spokesperson for Civil Rights.

9. Bid Whist is a partners' card game that is very popular in African American culture and is thought by some to have been developed during the time of slavery. The game consists of bidding to win hands or "books." If a team wins all 13 books they are said to have "run a Boston."

10. The Little Rock Nine were the nine teenagers who integrated Central High School in Little Rock Arkansas in 1957,

with support from the federal government. They are the subject of several documentaries and books.

11. Heaven Sutton was killed by a stray bullet in Chicago on June 27, 2012. She was seven years old.

12. In "On the Passing of Heaven Sutton" Shine on Me is known by the author as performed by Rev. James Cleveland. The origins of the song are thought to be a complex interplay of America's different folk traditions.

About the Author

Afaa M. Weaver did his graduate work in creative writing at Brown University after fifteen years as a factory worker in his native Baltimore. His awards in poetry include three Pushcarts and the Kingsley Tufts Award. In playwriting he received the PDI award from ETA Creative Arts Foundation. He teaches at Simmons College and in Drew University's MFA program. His official website is: www.afaaweaver.net

Author photo credit: Rachel Eliza Griffiths

www.ingramcontent.com/pod-product-compliance
Lightning Source LLC
Chambersburg PA
CBHW060344080526
44584CB00013B/913